I0707239

# TWO DOGS, TWO GRIEFS

**Debra J. Bilton**

Copyright © 2019 Debra J. Bilton

ISBN: 978-1-64718-140-6

All rights reserved. No part of this publication may be reproduced, stored in a retrieval system, or transmitted in any form or by any means, electronic, mechanical, recording or otherwise, without the prior written permission of the author.

Published by BookLocker.com, Inc., St. Petersburg, Florida.

Printed on acid-free paper.

Booklocker.com, Inc.
2019

# Preface

The past year or so of my life has been the worst I've ever endured. The stress of being a dementia caregiver while working at a small company that went through several major changes took its toll on me. I thought I was handling everything, my body and brain thought otherwise. Thrown into the mix, I was trying to keep an elderly, sick, then lame, then dying dog alive. At one point, for a while, I didn't know if or when I would recover. I lost a dog, my father, my physical health, cognitive abilities, and income. I hit the wall and was put on medical leave. I wouldn't wish what I went through on my worst enemy.

I feel like I've been to hell and back. The good news is, I made it back. A little tattered and torn, a bit worse for the wear, and yet I made it back. If it's true, that what doesn't kill you makes you stronger, then I must be Wonder Woman by now. I've regained my health and continue with brain training to create new neural pathways to improve my cognitive functioning. Most importantly, I've regained my resiliency and self-confidence.

After my dog died, I had the idea to write a book. I gave myself two years to do the research and finish writing it. I decided to self-publish through Booklocker.com. On a whim, I answered a trivia question from their affiliate website and won a free book publishing package. I was in shock. Not being one to look a gift horse in the mouth, and after my panic subsided, I took on this challenge. I would complete and submit a manuscript within a month, rather than within the twelve months I had given myself.

This is not how I had envisioned my first book. It was going to be filled with a lot of data, research findings, and interviews. After I won the package, I realized I would need to start writing a different book. It was going to be mostly my thoughts and feelings on having lost two dogs and how I grieved each differently. The shorter time frame changed the focus of my writing. As I wrote, I found my purpose wasn't just to tell a story and recount events, but to process what happened and understand it better. It would be more personal and intimate.

It kept changing as I moved through the writing process. My mind is like the annoying child who keeps asking why, why, why? I feel as though my life has passed before my eyes, in a good way, during the writing of this book. Memories and experiences from throughout my life have been connecting and coalescing to form a deeper, more meaningful understanding. Perhaps this is how my first book was meant to be.

# Acknowledgments

I am grateful to my best friend, Fawn Atherton, for your constant support and sometimes verbal kicks in the butt I need from time to time. I don't like hearing them and I always appreciate them upon reflection. You help me to see the world from a different perspective.

I thank Dr. Larry Landsborough for giving me your honest opinion. It helped me to make one of the best decisions I have ever made. What followed was meant to be.

I thank my older brother, Vaughn Bilton, for helping me with the final leg of Toby's journey. Your strength, physically and emotionally, helped me more than you will ever know.

And to my friend, Janice Carney, I thank you for sharing your home and your beloved pets with me. You were the port in the storm I needed every now and then.

# Table of Contents

# Introduction

In just under six years, I lost two beloved dogs. The first, Farley, was my heart and soul in a canine body. The second was Toby. Each of their deaths changed me. Hence, the reason for my writing this book. My hope was to learn why I grieved the loss of each so differently so that I can find meaning in their deaths and become a better person for it.

Throughout my lifetime I have, for the most part unconsciously, worked on processing my emotions to understand why I think and feel the way I do. A few years ago, my best friend asked me why I kept remembering and talking about difficult and sometimes traumatic events from the past. I paused to think about this, then replied, "I need to understand why they happened so that I can let them go."

This is how I learn my life lessons. I'm not always good at dealing with my emotions during the experience. I tend to push them down. I know this is not healthy and over time they demand your attention. When this happens, I look back to the event and break it down. I look at the details from different angles and perspectives. Inevitably I have an AHA moment where everything comes together and I understand what I was meant to learn. Then I can let it go and not carry the emotional burden anymore.

Farley's death almost broke me. I had never experienced such pain and loss. I was unprepared to deal with it. After almost six years, it took the death of Toby to help me finish grieving the loss of Farley. And for that, I am grateful to Toby.

When I told people that Toby had died, many had tears in their eyes and some cried. Although I had lost Toby, it was I who hugged and consoled them. I realized that many people who have lost their pets have not completely grieved their loss. Basically, people suck at grieving the loss of a pet. I know I did with Farley. It was different with Toby. The circumstances and the way he died were different.

When Farley died, I searched the internet for resources to help me through the grieving process. I found very little that helped. After Toby died, I found more useful resources, but not exactly what I needed. Hopefully what I have written here will be of use to someone who is grieving the loss of their pet.

# Farley

## The One

I wasn't sure how to start the story of my life with Farley. He was with me for just over fourteen years. He was the third dog in my life. And regardless of how many dogs you have, there is always that one, the one that touches your heart so deeply that you didn't know you could love a dog so much. For me, Farley was and always will be, the one.

Oddly enough, he started out as the dog I never wanted in my life. I wasn't looking forward to the puppy coming into the house. I had a fear of dogs since childhood, that I would push down and then it would rear its ugly head again and again, for many years. There were some periods where it reached the level of a phobia. I dealt with it as best as I could, but it limited my life in so many ways. I guess the universe gives us what we need when we're ready for it.

He was so small. I hadn't been around a puppy in years. He was also the first dog we had who lived inside the house. There were a lot of firsts with Farley, which was a steep learning curve for me. Dog training resources were not plentiful back then. I found a book at the local library that was written by Barbara Woodhouse. This is where I learned how to crate and potty train a puppy. I also think that her book is what started me on the journey of learning about dogs and how to work with them.

His crate was in the kitchen. That's where he slept at night, alone. At first, he would cry and whine when he woke up through the night. I couldn't lie in bed listening to him. It tore at my heartstrings. I'd read or heard somewhere that an animal will not do its business where it sleeps. Farley proved that this was not true.

When I'd go out to him, his bedding was sopped with urine, every single time. I'd take him out of his crate, clean him, replace his bedding, and then try to get him to sleep. I found that holding him against my heart while rocking and chanting Buddhist prayers and sutras worked the best. I'd wait until he was sound asleep to put him back into his crate. If I did it too soon, he would wake and cry, and the process would start again. Eventually, he slept through the night.

## Farley and the Fear

I was teaching my classes four nights a week and working double shifts every weekend at the racetrack. Everyone else in the house worked full-time days. I spent my days with Farley. This was a new experience for me. It was also difficult for me because of my fear of dogs. Most of the time I could rationalize the fear away, but emotions are irrational. They come when they want and keep doing so until you deal with them.

I clearly remember standing inside the back patio door. I looked at Farley, and something about seeing his face in profile triggered my fear. This visual must have been similar to a memory I had of the incident in my childhood that created my fear. For some reason, I knew this time was different. I'd always felt a general fear in the past, but this time I made a specific connection to a picture in my mind. Something inside of me told me to let the fear rise, and I did. I felt the fear in every cell of my body, the discomfort, and dread. After I'd experienced it completely, it left me. The new space created in my mind was gradually filled with my love for Farley.

Throughout this experience, Farley stood quietly and patiently beside me. In the past, I'd had dogs try to attack me when they sensed my fear. Not Farley. He waited. I didn't have a perception of time during this. It was like a meditation when you enter timeless time. There's no time or space. Just being. When it was done we went outside and continued on with our day.

Looking back I see that Farley was a therapy dog for me. And this happened years before I'd heard of this term. What he gave me that day was a gift and I am grateful to him. Years later I was able to give this gift to another dog. I paid it forward.

## More Steep Learning Curves

I had so many new experiences with Farley. I learned about the importance of confining a puppy to the back seat of the car while I was driving. I really didn't understand the inquisitive nature of puppies and their lack of knowledge about the world. I was naive. The first time I had Farley in the car with me I was shocked when he crawled under my legs and was entwined with my feet while I was driving. Somehow I got him out and ended up holding him against me with one arm. Our first car ride was a disaster. We both made it home safe and sound, and I knew I needed to change this arrangement.

When I don't understand something or lack knowledge, I research a topic to the point of becoming a semi-expert. I need to find answers to all of my questions. I guess my mind is like an inquisitive puppy. After reading a lot of information online, I decided that Farley needed a harness and I needed the attachment where one end clicked into the seat belt attachment and the other clipped onto the harness. He would be tethered into the back seat. This would give him a free rein of movement in the back seat and keep him from getting underfoot, literally.

Now the search was on. I went to several pet supply stores and found that this was not a popular item at the time. I went into the store at the mall and asked the woman working there if they sold this product. She said yes and then proceeded to tell me a story told to her by another customer.

The customer had recently bought the attachment to secure her large German Shepherd in the back of her car. She had a serious accident while driving and fortunately she and the dog were not injured. The police officer told her that it was a good thing she had her dog tethered in the back of the car. Otherwise, the impact of the accident would have thrown the dog forward. The forward motion, combined with the dog's weight, would have thrown him and her through the front windshield. This was the confirmation I needed. I bought the attachment with peace of mind.

My having all the right equipment wasn't a guarantee that I would use them correctly. I'd read that socializing puppies was really important, so I decided to take Farley to the church where I taught some of my classes. I'd called the secretary beforehand and she was looking forward to our visit. Once again, I didn't have a lot of knowledge about puppies and I was not using my logical reasoning skills on this day. I got out of the car, opened the rear door on the driver's side and unclipped the tether from Farley's harness. I should have clipped the leash onto his collar or harness before unclipping the tether. Here was a little, curious, energy-filled puppy with nothing attached to him. He was a free agent in the world.

I was shocked when he bounded out of the car and into the parking lot. To say that I felt panic was an understatement. He was so young he didn't know his name yet and wasn't trained for recall. And there were four lanes of traffic beside the church. I didn't want to run toward him in case it scared him or he thought I was playing and then ran away. I slowly walked toward him and talked to him in a calm voice. I only had seconds to get to him and I knew he could run faster than me.

And then a miracle happened. He stopped to sniff a worm in a puddle in the middle of the parking lot. All of his attention was focused on this little worm. Farley didn't even notice that I clipped the leash on him. The crisis was averted. I was so grateful to that little worm. And the secretary loved meeting Farley.

## The Gazelle

As Farley got older, he was allowed to be unsupervised in the fenced backyard. I knew he was safe out there and it gave him time to explore and just be a dog. A new water well was being drilled in the backyard. The work crew had taken down one section of the fence and temporarily replaced it with a piece of snow fencing. This allowed them easy access to the backyard with their heavy equipment. They weren't there that day, so I let Farley out. Never underestimate the curiosity of a young dog. It's always best to think two steps ahead of them. The snow fence was new and different. It probably carried the scent of the men who put it up. Of course, this would need to be thoroughly investigated by a scent oriented animal.

After a while, I went out to check on Farley. I didn't see him so I called his name and waited. No Farley. That was unusual. Unless he was around the other side of the back of the house where he couldn't hear me or was distracted. I started to walk in that direction when I caught movement out of the corner of my left eye. I turned to see one of the most beautiful sights I have ever seen in my life.

Two doors down, a dog was running in an empty field. I have never seen a dog so happy. Its front legs would stretch to reach their limit before barely touching the ground and the hind legs would quickly follow. It was a full out run using its body movements to the extreme. It was like watching a gazelle on an episode of the Mutual of Omaha's Wild Kingdom. I stood still for seconds, entranced by what I saw.

And then it hit me. That wasn't a dog, it was Farley. He must have jumped on the snow fence and not being sturdy it gave way and created an escape route for him. The fence was now in an upright position so it must have snapped back into place after he'd pushed it down. I opened the gate and started running toward the end of the field he was running in. This end was closest to the highway. I thought I could head him off at the pass.

He saw me as I was halfway to my intended destination. He stopped and looked at me. I could tell that he was wondering if he was in trouble. I didn't want him to run, especially with three lanes of traffic on the highway. I decided to make a game of it. I used my happy, hey buddy voice and motioned for him to come to me. He hesitated, and I continued. I wanted him to know that coming to me was a good thing. I needed for him to make that association. And it worked. He ran to me as fast as he could. I took hold of his collar and told him what a good boy he was. I kept praising him all the way home. After that, his backyard jaunts were supervised until the regular fence was reinstalled.

## The Red Rocket

Farley could run like the wind. His speed and grace astounded me. And the sheer joy that emanated from him filled me with awe and wonder. He was a reddish, brown blur as he raced around the backyard. He always ran the same route, up the side of the hill by the compost pile, across the top along the fence of the farmer's field, leaping down the side where the grapevines grew, and across the flat lawn at the bottom of the hill. He would complete this circuit over and over until he wore himself out.

I learned the hard way to not move when he ran by me. He could perfectly gauge how close he could get to me as he whizzed by and not make contact with me. I think it was a game for him. If I moved a fraction of an inch on his way by, he would smack into my legs. Sometimes it was just a graze, and other times it was a collision. It was difficult to stand still while watching him run toward me. I curbed my natural instinct to move for self-preservation. Over time, I came to trust his accuracy. He never made the slightest contact with me if I remained still.

Since he enjoyed running so much, I tried to play fetch with him. Unfortunately, he had a mind of his own and we played by his rules. I would throw the ball and he'd chase after it. He'd pick it up off the ground and come running back to me. I tried to teach him to give it to me, but that usually ended in a tug of war over the ball. Then I taught him to drop it. This worked well when he wanted to play. When he came running back to me with the ball, he would drop it beside me and keep running. Then he'd wait until I threw it again.

When he was done playing he would pick up the ball, go as far away from me as he could get, and then drop it. I could tell him to bring it back to me until I was blue in the face. No amount of coaxing or cajoling would entice him to play after that. When he was done, he was done.

And the best running story was told over and over by my father. He was in the backyard and saw Farley chasing a rabbit across the top of the back hill. Farley must have bit the rabbit because it squealed. Then he saw them both airborne as they launched from the top of the hill. The rabbit got away and Farley had enjoyed the chase.

## Bunnies and a Soft Mouth

The next day, Farley and I were walking in the backyard. He sniffed something at the bottom of the hill and then picked it up in his mouth. He didn't bite it or eat it. He very gently picked it up in his mouth. I told him to drop it and he did. I crouched down to get a closer look at the object. It was a baby rabbit. It was so young that it couldn't move much on its own yet. I looked up and saw the rabbit's nest halfway up the hill. The baby must have somehow fallen out and rolled down the hill.

I remembered hearing that you should not get your scent on a baby animal or the mother would reject it. I used the bottom of my shirt to pick it up and I gently placed it back into the nest with the other babies. Farley had come with me. I told him to leave the baby bunnies alone, and he did. He stayed a few feet back from the nest.

I made the connection that the rabbit Farley had chased was the mother. I was concerned that she was too injured to come back to her nest, or worse, she was dead. I found the phone number for a wildlife rescue group. I called to ask their advice on what to do to save the baby rabbits. I was surprised when the woman I talked to said that if the babies were still alive, then the mother was coming to care for them when no one was around. She must have cared for them at night because I never saw her during the day.

Every morning, Farley and I would go out and check on the bunnies. I reminded him to leave them alone. I would stand at the bottom of the hill while he walked a wide circle around the nest. He would sniff around but not get too close to the nest.

Then one morning we went to check the nest, and it was empty, except for one little rabbit that was dead. I'll never know if another animal got them, or if the mother was able to take most of them away. I hoped for the latter.

## Dogs and Energy

Reiki is a Japanese term that means life force energy, or energy of the soul. All living creatures have ki or qi, which is the energy that moves through us. According to Traditional Chinese Medicine, this energy moves through pathways known as meridians. If this energy is moving as it should, we have good health. If it is sluggish or blocked, we have ill health. Reiki is a method of healing that balances the energy of the body. An imbalance of energy can result in illness or be the result of injury.

I've shared Reiki with people and animals. I find that animals are more sensitive to it and are very honest in showing their need for it, especially dogs. If a dog is healthy and you try to give them Reiki, they will get up, give you the stink eye and walk away. That's honesty. If they are ill or injured, they will lie there and sleep until they have received enough energy to help them.

There was a partial fence at the top of the hill that was originally intended to be a part of a pen for Farley to live in. He ended up living indoors with us. One winter day, I was out back with him. He was doing his red rocket run and then I heard him yelp. He must have slipped on the snow or ice and hit his right hip against one of the fence posts. I ran up the hill to get to him. I knew it was bad because he wouldn't walk on his own and his whole body was trembling. I was worried he was going into shock.

I finally coaxed him down to the bottom of the hill. When we got there, he laid down with his injured hip on the snow. As soon as I saw him do this, I knew he was easing his pain with the coldness of the snow. It was the same as people using an ice pack on an injury. This would also reduce any swelling. Animals are so smart. I stayed with him until he was able to get up and walk again.

We went inside and he laid on the living room carpet with his injured hip exposed. I sat with my legs on either side of his body and proceeded to give him Reiki. His hip was so warm to the touch and it radiated energy. This told me he had injured it badly. I gave him Reiki for about half an hour and visualized cooling the affected area with the element of water. Then I used the white light to heal the area. He had a deep, restful sleep after that. Then he was fine.

There were times I would try to give Reiki to Farley when he was curled up, sound asleep in his bed. There was nothing wrong with him. I was curious to see how he would respond. His reaction was the same every time. He would wake up and give me a look that let me know he was not impressed. Then he would get up, walk into another room and lie down. He just wanted to get away from me so he could sleep in peace.

These little experiments taught me that animals have an innate sense of this energy. They know when they're energy bodies are balanced, and they know when they're not.

## Birds, Too

I have also given Reiki to birds. Hey, I'll share the energy with any living being that needs and will benefit from it. Years ago we had a budgie that had a stroke. I can't remember its name because we had so many budgies over the years. One morning I found him at the bottom of his cage. He was alive but couldn't move. I suspected he had a stroke, as most budgies do as they near the end of their life. I gave him Reiki and after a few minutes he started moving. Shortly after that, he was back to his normal self. He lived for another two months.

Years later I tried the same thing with another budgie, Sparks, but wasn't able to help her. I came home from work one night and found her lying on the bottom of her cage. I gave her Reiki over and over again. Then I accepted that this would not help her. The stroke must have caused too much damage to her brain.

I remember her being very friendly after her stroke. Prior to that, she was content to be in her cage all the time. After the stroke, she wanted to be with me all the time when I was home. So, I carried her around in my hand when I went through the house.

I had to make disability-related accommodations to her cage for when I was at work. She couldn't get up to her regular water and food dishes. And if I placed them on the floor of her cage, she still couldn't reach them. I tried different types of small dishes and bowls but they weren't the right height and weight.

I needed a water dish that was high enough for her to lean her head into to drink from it, but not so low that she would fall into it and drown. The food dish needed to be low enough for her to lean her head into to eat, and heavy enough to not tip over and onto her when she leaned into it with her body weight. Thank goodness for dollar stores. I found two square, shallow, porcelain dishes that met these conditions.

When I was home, I made a nest out of an old sweatshirt and put it on the bed beside me. She would sleep in it or in the curve of my neck while I read or worked on the computer. At night, she slept in the sweatshirt nest beside me. She lived for a couple of weeks after her stroke.

# Farley and Toby

## Becoming a Towny Dog

About halfway through Farley's life, we moved from a rural area into a townhouse in town. The house we'd previously lived in was a bungalow so the only stairs were to the basement. The townhouse had two separate sets of stairs. I remember my legs were so sore for the first week after going up and down the stairs.

Farley fared better than I did, except for the first night. He couldn't make it up the stairs to go to bed. I think I had to hook my arm under his chest and help him with each stair. He was so exhausted. And after I helped him up the stairs, I was exhausted. We all slept well the first night in the new home.

Other than when we went camping, Farley hadn't walked on a leash. He ran free in the backyard. As he got older, he slowed down and was gaining weight. It turned out that my learning to walk him on a leash in town helped him to lose weight and his body toned up. It did the same for me, so it was a win-win situation. He wore a harness, and I used a Flexi leash. I wouldn't use either of these with most dogs, but they worked with Farley because he was easy to leash train.

I had to reinforce the basic commands of stop, sit and stay. There was heavy traffic where we now lived and several crosswalks that we used. The hardest thing about walking Farley was not letting him greet every human being that he saw. He was well socialized with people, very gentle and friendly. I also understood that not everyone likes dogs, so I would wait until the person indicated that they wanted to interact with Farley.

A good example of this was the elderly, war veteran who would drive his scooter in our direction, park it beside Farley and then proceed to talk to him and pet him. I met a lot of people on our walks, and quite frankly people were more interested in talking to the dog than me. Who could blame them? It's hard to resist eighty pounds of love.

I was looking forward to greeting and meeting the neighbors in the complex. At first, people were friendly from a distance, but they didn't seem keen on meeting Farley. Then I realized it was probably because he was the biggest dog in the neighborhood. Over time people must have realized that he was a laid back, happy-go-lucky, friendly dog. He didn't bark at people or jump on them. He was very respectful in the way he greeted and interacted with people. Even people who were afraid of dogs were won over by Farley. It must have been that therapy dog thing he had going for him.

## Co-Pilot

Although I walked him a lot around where we lived, Farley was in the car with me a lot more. I took him everywhere with me. Other than hot days, I'd leave him in the car with the windows partially down while I ran into stores or did other errands. He was quite content to sit alone in the car. I've seen some dogs who sit in the car and stare at the door of the building their owner just went into. They will not break their intense gaze until they see their owner come out through the same door.

This was not the case with Farley. Most of the time when I walked back to my car, he was looking in any direction other than the one he'd seen me go in. He was so busy watching people that the sight of my appearance or the sound of my opening the car door would startle him slightly. Then he'd resume his regular car dog position, with his rear end sitting on the back seat, front paws on the floor and his upper body wedged between the two front bucket seats. He was my co-pilot when I was driving.

Actually, that's not true. He was the co-pilot to whoever was driving my car. I would take him with me when I took my car in to be serviced at the auto mechanics. One of the guys would drive us back home in my car and then take it back to be serviced. Farley would always lean on and give his full attention to the guy driving my car. It always struck me as odd that he didn't care that a stranger was driving it. I guess he was loyal to the driver, not me. And I think the guys kind of liked it. Farley had this way with people that I can't quite explain.

## And Then There Were Two

Shortly after Farley became a towny dog, Toby came into my life, indirectly at first. He was the new puppy who now belonged to my parents. For the first few months, my mother would drop him off to stay with me during the day because puppies have small bladders and can't be left alone for long. I taught at night and worked weekends, so this was a good arrangement.

I remember that Farley was initially curious about Toby. He wanted to sniff him and check him out. Later the curiosity was replaced with avoidance. Toby's exuberance became too much for Farley. Older dogs can only take so much from puppies. What is playtime for a puppy can be harassment to an older dog. I learned to use baby gates to separate them.

When Toby was really young, I would gate him into the kitchen. I needed to keep him safe and containing him seemed to be the best strategy. When he was teething he would chew anything and everything, including electrical cords. I was always worried that he was going to fall down the stairs, or even worse, through the rails beside the stairs.

As he grew older and bigger my concerns for his safety lessened. He learned how to get up and down the stairs. Next came racing up and down the stairs. Oh, he was so much fun and a handful at the same time. One time I was looking for him upstairs and found him squatting in my room. Shouting, "NO!" had little effect. It was too late. When nature calls you have to answer. He wasn't completely house trained yet and there was no way he could have made it down two flights of stairs and outdoors in time. It only happened that once.

Their temperaments were so different as puppies. I remembered that Farley would run around and play, and then all of a sudden he would drop to the floor in a deep sleep. It was odd to watch because it wasn't a gradual tiring. After sleeping for a while he'd be up and on the go again, until the next time he dropped into dreamland.

Toby, on the other hand, would just get tired and cranky. It was as though he wouldn't give in to his tiredness and go to sleep. He kept going and going. He was not an enjoyable companion at these times. I would have to put him in his crate or gate him in the kitchen and leave him alone. If he was alone, and it was quiet, he would sleep.

I would either let Toby or Farley out into the backyard, one at a time. Later Farley would be loose and I'd keep Toby on the leash. I let Farley decide how close he wanted to get to Toby. I didn't want to force the issue. Farley was well socialized with people, but not with dogs. I let him set the pace with other dogs.

## Problems?

When my sister came home from work, we would walk both dogs on leashes. Farley needed the exercise and Toby needed to burn off his excess energy. It also helped them to be close to each other outside of the house. They could be side by side, distracted by the myriad of new scents along the way. At times, Farley would try to get closer to Toby until Toby would lunge at him. It was playful puppy behavior and Farley was having none of that.

Toby completely trusted Farley throughout his time in Farley's life. I'd go so far as to say he adored Farley. The feelings were not mutual. For the most part, Farley tolerated Toby and his wild behavior. That was Farley's way with animals and people.

The first indication of Toby's severe behavioral problems came during one of our walks. We had just finished walking over a bridge. I saw a man walking toward us on the sidewalk. As he approached us Toby became aggressive. He was barking, snarling and lunging at the man. We were able to restrain him with the leash and no harm was done. I was surprised at his behavior and the ferocity of it. This was a portent of things to come.

## Unknown Origins

Farley was a relaxed and happy puppy. Toby, on the other hand, was always on alert. I realize now that it was due to his having two herding breeds in his genetic makeup, Border Collie and Australian Shepherd. He supposedly also had Spitz in him and came from a breeder. If a dog is a mixture of breeds, it didn't come from a breeder. It's a mutt.

I suspect Toby came from a puppy mill. He was kept in a penned area of a room in a woman's house. And there were other mixed breed puppies of different ages in the pen. The woman told my parents she was selling them for a breeder. She also told them the puppies had never been outside because they hadn't had their vaccinations yet. My take on that was she didn't let them outside because she didn't want the neighbors to see the business she was running out of her home.

Toby was nervous, high-strung and unusually bold for a puppy. I wonder how much of this was due to genetics and how much was a result of his fending for himself in a pen with other puppies from different litters. He probably didn't have much contact with people either. He lacked proper socialization with dogs and people. He didn't have a lot in his favor from the start.

## Taming of the Wild Thing

As Toby got older, he could stay alone at my parents' house. I would go there to check on him and let him outside to run and do his business. When he was five or six months old, I did something I never thought I would do to a dog and I've never done it again. When I was outside with him, he kept biting me. I brought him inside and he continued to bite me. He didn't break the skin, but it hurt and I wanted him to stop doing it. Nothing that I said or did influenced his behavior.

Finally, I pinned him down on the living room floor. When I did this he fought like a wild animal caught in a trap. I knew that once I had him in that position I couldn't let him go until we had finished and reached an agreement. If I let him up before that he would have bitten me again.

My purpose wasn't to dominate him. Personally, I think the dominance theory for dogs is a fallacy. It came from an artificially created environment where adult wolves were taken from their different families and forced to live together with strangers. The experiment that led to this theory is similar to a reality television show where people live with strangers in a house together. The difference is the wolves had no choice in the matter, no fun games to play, and no prizes to win at the end of it all. This would not happen in nature. Families of wolves live together in harmony. The unnatural environment forced them to fight for survival, and dominance was needed for survival.

My intention for Toby was to wait patiently until he relaxed. I didn't want him to give in to me or give up. I didn't want to take anything away from him. I wanted to give him the experience of trusting a human. To do this, I needed him to move through his fear and aggression, and then come to a knowing that he was not hurt by this. He was safe.

It's a good thing I'm a martial artist and know about feigning. At times Toby would lie still, panting with exhaustion. I knew he was either resting for the next round or pretending to relent. If I eased up then, I knew he would fight against me again. I could feel the tension in his body and see the whale eyes, where his eyes were wide and I could see the whites. Sometimes his eyes would flick to the corner to look at me. I knew he was assessing me, to see if I was ready to release him. He tried everything he knew to do, but this was a completely new experience for him.

I was exhausted, and the sweat was pouring down my face and body. I would reposition my hands to adjust to the thrashing movements of his body. And the whole time I calmly talked to him in a soothing voice. I refused to give up on him because I knew he was worth all the effort.

It took half an hour. As I waited, I felt the tension leave his body and I saw his eyes become soft. That was when I knew we had reached an agreement. I no longer needed to use my hands to restrain his body. Now I used them to pet and caress his body. I praised him over and over.

Our relationship changed dramatically after that. He wanted to be with me and to interact with me. He never again tried to bite me for no reason. I think that was when the seeds of trust were planted for each of us.

## Camping: Good For One, Not the Other

Farley was the best camping dog ever. He never barked at anyone or disturbed the peace in any way. He was content to lie in the sun and sleep for hours during the day. I'd take him for a long walk in the morning and early evening. And he loved to wade in the lake. He wasn't one to swim, he just wanted to stand in the water. Those were good times.

And then Toby came camping with us. He was about seven months old the first time he went. All was going well on the first day until a dog ran at him barking. Dogs were supposed to be on a leash or tied up in the campsite. This one was not and its owner had no control over it. Toby wanted to defend himself but he was restrained by the leash. His fear of and aggression toward other dogs escalated after that and stayed with him throughout his life. The exception for him was always Farley.

We continued to take Toby camping for a few years. I had hopes that he would calm as he aged. Part of the problem was that he lived on a rural property throughout the year where he had little exposure to other dogs. He was never socialized with other dogs.

Going camping once a year was very stressful for him. During the day he spent most of the time lying in his crate in the porch outside the camper. The crate was covered with towels or blankets to block his view of people walking by, especially people with dogs. Of course, that did not block his senses of smell and hearing. He would lash out with his fear and pent up energy. It was not a good experience for him.

The only exceptionally good experience I remember Toby having was the one time he swam in the lake. After we made sure there were no other dogs around, we took him and Farley down to the far end where dogs were allowed to swim. Farley, being the wader he was, just stood in the water while the waves lapped at his legs and body.

Toby, on the other hand, took to the water like a duck. He was tentative at first because this was new to him. When he got far enough into the water that his body was covered, it was like a switch was turned on inside of him. He just wanted to swim and swim. We let him go out as far as he could on the leash. If it was up to him, he would have swam to the middle of the lake and back. He was in water heaven, and he slept well that night.

Eventually, Toby was left at home when my parents went camping. My sister and I would take turns staying with him. One of us would stay at the house with Toby, and the other went camping with Farley and our parents. This was the best way we found to manage the situation. It was less stressful for everyone.

## Crate and Rotate

Whenever I took Farley to my parents' house, I always insisted they be separated by a baby gate. Farley was usually in the kitchen and Toby had the run of the rest of the house. Now and then I would put Toby in his crate so Farley could have the run of the house. It was a lesser version of the crate and rotate strategy that some dog owners use when there are aggression issues between dogs. I wasn't concerned about Farley being aggressive in any way. My concern was with Toby. I didn't trust him and I had seen him lash out at Farley with misplaced aggression during a camping trip.

When Farley wanted to come out of the kitchen, he would hang his head over the baby gate, looking into the hall. Whenever he did this, Toby would sneak up and touch his nose to Farley's. Farley didn't like that and would back away from the gate.

After a while, I'd put Toby in his crate and let Farley out. Toby didn't mind being in the crate. He would lie there and his eyes would follow every movement that Farley made. This was one of the few times that Farley felt comfortable going up to Toby. He would look at him and sniff him through the bars of the crate.

People would tell me to let the dogs be together and work it out. For me, that would have been irresponsible. Neither dog had been socialized with other dogs when they were puppies. The optimal time for this is between three and fourteen to sixteen weeks of age. The window of opportunity had been missed for each of them. Farley was not aggressive toward other dogs, but his lack of social skills annoyed other dogs. He wanted to sniff and not be sniffed. Toby was aggressive. He had not been socialized with dogs, or with people.

As time went by, I closed one of my class locations and started working in an office during the day. Toby was not much a part of my life after that. He was an adult dog and could be left alone in the house while my parents were at work. I would see him occasionally on weekends when I visited.

I wish I knew then what I know now about Toby. If I had taken the time to become more knowledgeable about dog behavior and patiently used that knowledge to work with Toby, it could have been a different outcome. Perhaps I could have helped him more.

## Mama Bear

I've never had children, so I didn't know what it felt like to be fiercely protective of another until the night of the attack. It was Christmas Eve, and we were returning home from our nightly walk with Farley. There was a German Shepherd in the complex that was extremely fear aggressive toward other dogs and its owners could barely hold on to its leash. I made a point of avoiding them on our walks. On this night, as we were walking past the house where the Shepherd lived, its owners came home and opened their front door. I looked and saw there was no inside door and the Shepherd was standing in the doorway.

In mere seconds it laser focused its attention on Farley and made a beeline for him. It happened so fast and the dog didn't make a sound. Farley didn't see it coming. Fortunately, I'm good in a crisis. I assess, decide and then act. It comes from decades of martial arts training. I did a quick visual scan and realized the owners were frozen in place. I knew they would do nothing to intervene. They would wait until their dog had finished its attack on Farley and then try to get their dog away.

I looked and saw the Shepherd had pinned Farley against a snow bank and the Shepherd was on top of him. I could barely see Farley because the other dog was bigger than him. I knew Farley had no way to defend himself or to escape. Assessment done, decision made, now to act. I threw myself on top of the Shepherd and kept pounding it with my right fist while shouting, "No!" I kept hearing yelps and I thought they were coming from Farley. This made me more determined to save him.

Then everything changed. The yelping stopped and I felt my weight shift. Then I was on my knees and put my palms on the ground for support. I looked up and saw the Shepherd's face a few inches in front of mine. That was the only moment when I thought that I may have made a bad decision. The dog and I stared into each other's eyes. Then it ran around and behind me to its owners. I pushed myself up off the ground and saw Farley standing with my sister.

We immediately started toward home. I was worried that Farley was injured, but I wanted to get him away from there first to ensure his safety. I could see his harness and fur were disheveled. I could also see by the way he was moving that he was disoriented. I was concerned that he might be in shock.

We got him into the house and I immediately ran my hands over his entire body to do a quick check for injuries. First aid training for people also comes in handy for pets. I found nothing overt. My next concern was he might have puncture wounds if the other dog bit him, which could lead to an infection. I ran upstairs and came back down with a white washcloth. I methodically wiped it over his body, stopping periodically to see if there was blood on the cloth. There was none.

He didn't seem to be physically injured, but he was badly shaken up. I guess I'd be shaken up too if I was peacefully walking one minute and then slammed to the ground with a dog on top of me the next. And I'm sure my extra weight on top of the Shepherd made it worse for Farley.

After calming him, I sat back and looked at Farley. He was alright. Then I realized that it was his harness that prevented him from being injured. The Shepherd must have bit into the harness. My throwing my body into the foray was probably distraction enough for the Shepherd to not release its grip on the harness and then bite Farley.

The owners of the Shepherd never came to ask if Farley was okay. Later I learned that their dog had attacked another dog in the complex and injured it. This attack happened before the one with Farley, so I know Shepherd could have hurt Farley. I saw them walking the

Shepherd the next morning and it appeared to be fine. The owners moved out of the complex within a couple of months. I was relieved.

From this incident, I learned that I will fiercely protect those that I love, without a thought about my personal safety. Years later I learned that I will do this for any animal. Once the Mama Bear thing has been awakened, it doesn't go into hibernation. My protective instincts transferred to a dog I didn't even know.

I was on an annual walk for charity when I heard a dog furiously barking. I looked across the street and saw a small, white dog running toward the street. There was a large group of us walking and it was going to run across to us. I did a quick left and right scan of the street and when I saw a break in the traffic, I ran toward the dog. It kept barking at me, lunging toward me, and trying to bite me. It would run at me and then try to run around me. I kept dodging back and forth, using my open hands to block it from going onto the street. The whole time I kept saying, "Don't bite me. Please, don't bite me."

Then some women and girls of different ages came running out of a house. They were all running around and screaming. I quickly surmised the dog belonged to them. Unfortunately, their loud voices and attempts to physically get a hold of the dog added to the chaos. The dog would run to them, run away from them, and then run back to try to attack me. I decided to stay the course. I remained where I was, moving only to block the dog's attempts to get to the street. Finally, one of the women got a hold of the dog and picked it up. They thanked me and I left to rejoin my group of walkers.

### Fred

It was early morning and Farley and I were walking toward the backfield behind the complex. Our pace was leisurely and our walk was peaceful until I heard a woman's voice shouting "FRED! FRED!" I thought maybe Fred was a lost child. I turned to the direction of the voice and saw that Fred was a young Cocker Spaniel barreling full tilt down the hill directly toward us.

Farley was an elderly dog by then and enjoyed polite greetings with well-mannered dogs. Fred's unbridled exuberance dashed my hopes of a polite greeting in the next few seconds. As it turned out, it dashed Farley's hopes too. I attempted to use verbal commands and hand signals to stop Fred's onslaught, or at least slow him down. Fred was either unfamiliar with these commands and signals, or he just didn't care.

Poor Farley. Fred chased him in circles for what seemed like an eternity. Farley was on the Flexi leash, so his movements and space to run in were restricted. He kept running in a circle around me, where I was the focus, the center of his circle. I kept turning in the direction they were running to prevent Farley's leash from wrapping around me. They were moving so fast and I could see that Farley was panicking and tiring quickly. I kept shouting at Fred to stop, but he was having such a great time chasing Farley.

Finally, his owner came into view at the top of the hill. She called to him and he ran toward her. When she tried to grab his collar, he darted away and ran circles around her. Then he remembered us and started running in our direction again.

I'd had enough of Fred by this time. I quickly changed my body language. I stepped forward and took an assertive stance in front of Farley. I raised the palm of my hand and my voice toward Fred. This stopped him. After several attempts, his owner was able to get the leash on him. She apologized several times and each time I accepted her apology. I was glad to see them leave. Farley and I continued on our walk.

About a year later, Farley and I had finished walking in the same field. As we were exiting on the opposite side, I noticed a young girl walking on the sidewalk above us. At the time I didn't see the dogs she was walking with because my view of them was blocked the bridge. We continued our slow incline up the hill until I heard the girl shouting. She was too far away for me to hear what she was shouting. Then I saw movement, fast movement, coming toward us. It was Fred, barreling down the hill toward us.

Elderly dogs do not want or appreciate being chased by younger dogs. It's annoying and goes against the natural rhythm of nature. In the past year, I'd become more watchful and protective of Farley as age slowed him down. I would not allow another Fred circle chasing event.

I told Farley to stay and stood in front of him. When Fred was within about six feet of us, I pushed the palm of my hand toward him and firmly said, "STOP!" To my great surprise, he stopped and stood still. I don't know if Fred had received training over the past year or if it was my calm and assertive demeanor that influenced his behavior. I told him to stay and he did.

The girl came into view. She had two smaller dogs with her that were also off-leash. These two stood beside her and Fred just stood still looking at Farley and me. The girl called to Fred and he went to her. She and her three dogs walked away up the hill. I waited until they were out of view before I continued my walk with Farley.

I never saw Fred again. He was a happy, go-lucky, high energy dog. Under different circumstances, I would have enjoyed meeting him.

# The Ravages of Time

## Do You See What You See?

Sensei, my martial arts teacher, would often repeat the teaching, "Do you see what you see?" When it came to Farley aging and approaching the end of his life, I had blinders on. I didn't want to see what I was seeing. I adjusted my behavior to compensate for the losses that old age was inflicting upon him. I was shown in a dream that he would live to be fifteen years old. I kept that in the back of my mind, knowing I had another year with him.

On Mother's Day weekend, I was doing laundry and had the back patio door open so that Farley could go in and out as he pleased. I had just put clothes in the dryer when I heard a terrible screeching noise. I knew that an animal was being killed. I found out later that it was a hawk killing a rabbit behind the fence of the backyard.

I went to the doorway to see what was happening. I couldn't see the attack, but I did see the effect this noise had on Farley. It's difficult to describe. It was as though his eyes zoned out or unfocused, and then his head tilted to one side. Then he fell to the ground and was lying on the patio in a full seizure.

I called out to my sister who was upstairs, and she came down. I ran to get a blanket to put under his head. Every time his head hit the cement it made a sickening, thudding sound. I knew from my first aid training that I needed to protect his head from injury. Then it was a matter of waiting for the seizure to end. I have no idea of how long it went on for. It seemed like an eternity. My perception of time was clouded by my concern for Farley.

Finally, it ended. He was groggy and disoriented. When he was able to get up and walk, we helped him to get into the back room. I kept trying to get him to stand still, with the hope of then getting him to lie down to recover, but he just kept aimlessly wandering around. I had to use my arms as a cushion when he walked too close to the furniture and walls. It was as though he couldn't stand in one place, he had to keep moving.

Eventually, he settled down, and we were able to get him upstairs. He slept soundly through the night. He seemed better the next morning, but there was a fragility about him for the rest of his days. From one of our Buddhist prayers, he lost "the strong confidence that only robust health can bring."

## Some Things Get Harder With Age

When he was younger, I would take Farley to my Tai Chi classes. The students loved him. He was very interested in socializing with everyone. I only took him to class once when he was older. I was teaching at a different location so this would have been new to him. He was friendly with my students, but he didn't want to socialize with them this time. He kept wandering behind the stacks of chairs and tables at the far end of the room. He was constantly pacing and working himself up into a panicked state. I tried to calm him as best as I could during class and never took him there again.

One time I was driving and I heard a loud thud and then scrambling noises in the back of the car. I was driving so I couldn't fully turn around to see what had happened. I made a quick glance in the rearview mirror and over my right shoulder, but I couldn't see Farley. I pulled into a parking lot as soon as I could. I got out and opened the rear car door to see Farley lying on the floor. He couldn't get up by himself. I immediately got into the back with him and lifted him to a sitting position.

I looked down and saw the cup holder was opened. I think he fell and hit the edge of the cup holder which pulled it open. He was wedged between the bottom of the back seat and cup holder. He didn't have the agility or strength to extricate himself. As one of my students said to me, it sucks to get old.

Farley would moan when he got up or laid down. I knew he had arthritis. I also noticed that his muscles had wasted with age. The two flights of stairs in the townhouse got to be too much for him. I would help him walk up the stairs by hooking my forearm under his barrel chest and lift him. I was doing most of the work but his legs kept moving like he was walking. I wanted him to think he was doing the work because I didn't want to take away his dignity. When I lifted him, I could see his facial muscles ease. I could tell it greatly alleviated his pain. This gave me a sense of relief, peace and calm that his physical suffering was eased for a few minutes.

## Bucket List

My intuition must have told me that he would soon come to the end of his life. Once again, I was in denial about this. I didn't want to see it. Over the last two weeks of his life, I took him to all of his favorite walking places, and he had a lot of them. At the time I didn't know why I was doing this. I tried to convince myself that I just wanted him to have fun. Now I see that I had unconsciously made a bucket list for him.

After we moved to town, Farley had few opportunities to run free without a leash attached to him. I found one place where he could run. It was a fenced tennis court. I would keep Farley on the leash while I walked around and checked for broken glass or any other objects that could harm him. Then I would check that the gate was closed. Once I was sure the court was safe and secure, I'd unsnap the leash and tell him to run. The first few times he wasn't sure of what to do. That didn't last long. He learned quickly that this was a place of red rocket freedom. He loved it.

This was one of the last places I took him to from his bucket list. There was no red rocket running this time. He was too old and arthritic now. The best he could manage was a slow, gentle, loping motion. And I could see the look of joy on his face. I'm so glad I took him there one last time.

## An Unexpected Ending

As usual, I got up early to walk Farley before I went to work. I noticed that he was off that morning. His movements were slower and more difficult. I put the coat on him that I had recently purchased for him. He didn't have much fat on his body and his muscles were wasting. I wanted to keep him warm. I tried to shorten his walk to make it easier for him, but he was having none of that. So it took us a little longer than usual and that was okay. We went back home. I helped him up the stairs, got ready, and went to work.

It was New Year's Eve, and I was looking forward to only working a half a day. I finished at noon and decided to stop by the grocery store to pick up a few things, knowing everything would be closed the next day for the holiday. I got home, took my shoes off, looked up and saw my mother standing in the back room. I was surprised that she was there. She said something was wrong with Farley.

I immediately went into the backroom to see Farley lying on the carpet. Our eyes met, and I saw his body relax and release tension. Then he tried to get up and fell down. I tried to get him to lie down, but he kept trying to get up. I knew he had to go outside to do his business, and I needed to see how bad he was.

I put the harness on him so I could hold on to it to support him. I got him to the back door, put my arms under his chest and lifted him down onto the patio. I held onto his harness and helped him over to the snow bank, where he seemed to want to go. I let go for a moment to see how much mobility he had. He fell over to the side, against the snow bank. That told me everything. He couldn't walk because he had no control over his back legs.

I lifted him up and walked him, with my arms under his chest to support him. He peed. I supported him to the back door and then lifted him back into the house. He wanted a drink, so I held onto him while he drank. Then I helped him to the middle of the room to lie on the carpet. After that, I somehow put him into his crate where he could lie comfortably on his bed.

My mother told me that my sister and her husband heard Farley bark earlier in the morning and went downstairs to check on him. He had trouble walking at first but then was able to. They went back upstairs and later heard a noise and went back down to find he couldn't walk at all. I surmised from this information that he had two strokes. I knew the damage was permanent.

I didn't know what to do, so I started calling different veterinary clinics. It was 1:30 in the afternoon, the day before a holiday and most places had closed at noon. First I tried the veterinarian clinic Farley had been going to for the last few years. Closed. Then I tried the one he had gone to for the first part of his life. Closed. Then I started randomly calling clinics that I found online. Only one was open. They agreed to look at Farley but we had to wait to bring him in for an appointment.

I stayed downstairs with Farley. At one point I gave him some water and he threw it up. I cleaned him up and put puppy pee pads under his head so he would be comfortable. Now it was just waiting for the time to take him to the clinic. He slept most of the time as I sat with him.

When it was time for the appointment, my sister and I carried Farley out to the back of her vehicle. We stayed in the back with him while her husband drove. We carried him into the clinic where the veterinary technician said he needed to be weighed. I remember thinking, this is probably his last day on earth so why bother weighing him? I kept my thought to myself. After he was weighed we took him into an examination room, where we waited for the veterinarian.

The veterinarian came in and said that we needed to get Farley up onto the examination table. I said no because it would be too difficult for Farley. Eventually, he agreed to examine Farley where he was, lying on the floor. He got behind Farley and put his hands under his hips. He said that Farley was in a lot of pain from arthritis. For some reason that hit me hard. My first thought was, "Oh, Far." He must have been in excruciating pain for some time and he didn't show it. He didn't whine or yelp. He just carried on. Animals can be so stoic.

The veterinarian said that it was neurological. I asked if it was a stroke and he said yes. Farley also had a heart murmur. We took him out to the waiting room to discuss what to do next. I said he needed to be put down so he didn't suffer. That was so hard because he was alert and his personality was still there. I also knew the quality of his life would greatly suffer if he continued to live.

I suggested a mobile veterinarian to my sister, who would come to the house to euthanize Farley. The veterinarian at the clinic said that he could come to the house to do it, after he finished with another dog at the clinic. We agreed and took Farley home.

We got home and lifted Farley out of the vehicle. I held him up so he could have his last pee and then took him inside. We brought his favorite bed downstairs for him to lie on. I just stayed with him, lying on the side of his bed while I pet him and spoke softly to him. He slept on and off. The veterinarian had planned on coming to the house around 5:30 pm but ran late working with the other dog. I didn't mind. I had more time with Farley. It was peaceful.

The veterinarian and his technician arrived at the house after 6:30 pm. I'm not sure of the exact time. We moved Farley and his bed over a bit to give the veterinarian room to work with Farley. He injected the sedative into Farley's front leg and I saw Farley's body relax.

I was sitting beside his head and leaned down to whisper in his ear what I had told him throughout his life. I was surprised to see his tail wag because I thought he had lost his hearing a while back. It hit me then that he had been in so much pain with his arthritis that it took all of his attention to concentrate on his movements. He wasn't able to attend to auditory stimuli. The sedative relaxed his body and freed him from pain. That's why he could hear what I whispered to him.

As I sat up I saw tears streaming down the face of the veterinary technician. I don't think she was close enough to hear what I said to Farley. I sensed that she felt the emotions of that brief interaction between us.

Then the veterinarian made several attempts to inject Farley's front legs with the drug to euthanize him. Farley was so old that his veins had collapsed and the veterinarian said he would need to inject the drug into Farley's heart. Twice he told me it was best that I leave for this procedure, and twice I told him that I would not leave. Many years before, I had told Farley that I would love him always and forever, and I would be there for him until the end of his life. When you give your word, you keep it. It's a matter of integrity.

Farley was asleep as I was stroking his head and softly talking to him. At the moment the injection went in I saw his eyes and mouth fly wide open. It had missed his heart. The veterinarian immediately repeated the procedure and then Farley was gone. This happened in mere seconds. I looked up at the clock.

I learned afterward that this is an extremely difficult procedure to perform and it is the least preferred. It was further made difficult with a dog lying in a bed on the floor and poor lighting in the room.

Farley died on New Year's Eve 2012, at 7:20 pm.

Farley's fourteenth birthday was in October. He died in his fifteenth year of life.

# Toby

## An Old Dog New in My Life

I moved into my parents' house a few months after Farley died. And that was how I got to know Toby better. He had always been good with me up to that point. Then it just got better and better. Before it got better, it got a lot worse. Due to his aggressive behavior, Toby was kept at home most of the time. It was a rural area where he didn't have contact with other dogs, other than Farley who Toby had absolutely adored.

What I didn't know when I moved into my parents' house was that my father was in the early stages of dementia. I noticed his behavior was different from I'd known before, but thought he wasn't adjusting well to retirement. Over time, I learned the truth and our lives changed greatly. This was the beginning of the most difficult time of my life. Dementia is insidious and a thief. It stole so much from so many, especially from my father.

## The Dog Next Door

Toby was free to run in the part of the backyard that was fenced. He was fine with the neighbors on that side of the house. He would bark at them playfully and they didn't mind. It was a fairly peaceful situation until the neighbors got a puppy. Then everything in Toby's world changed.

My parents were away on a camping vacation. At first, I didn't know the neighbors had a dog. Toby would run around whining and barking and I couldn't figure why. Then I heard the puppy bark. I couldn't see it because the fence of the neighbor's backyard was solid. I started walking Toby on a leash in the backyard after that.

The first time Toby saw the puppy didn't go well. The neighbor had the puppy out front where Toby could see him through the chain-link fence. It took everything I had to hold on to the leash. Toby was growling, barking, pulling and lunging. I finally got him back into the house.

I've heard people say that an adult dog will not hurt a puppy. I've seen it with my own eyes and I know that is not true. A well-socialized and emotionally balanced adult dog would not hurt a puppy. Toby was neither of those. One day Toby was off-leash and saw the puppy on the other side of the chain-link fence. He ran at it in a frenzy, trying to attack it. If the fence wasn't there he would have hurt it badly. His level of aggression was frightening to see. Looking back, it was heartbreaking. It's not normal for a dog to behave that way and it's very stressful for them.

As the puppy next door grew into a dog, Toby's days of running free in the backyard came to an end. The barking and eventual aggression of both dogs toward each other escalated. This created tension in the household. It got to the point where I was the only one who would take him out to do his business. Many times I dreaded it. If the other dog was out, Toby wouldn't do his business. It was frustrating for Toby and me. I never blamed Toby for his behavior. I knew that he was doing the best he knew to do.

This led to my scheduling my life around the outside schedule of the dog next door. I was trying to create peace and harmony in a chaotic situation. I would wake up in the morning while it was still dark to feed Toby and then take him out front to do his business. This worked well most of the time. Occasionally the other dog was out and a lot of barking ensued.

My goal was to take care of Toby's basic needs without waking everyone up. I'd take Toby out at night before my parents went to bed so the barking dogs wouldn't wake them. Between morning and night, it was hit and miss. I'd just take my chances and hope for the best.

It was a crazy schedule and I could see that Toby was not happy. He wasn't getting much exercise and this led to a lot of pent up energy and frustration. It became a vicious cycle. His frustration would build until he had an opportunity to explode in an aggressive outburst. Oddly, he also seemed timid and eager to please people. I was trying to get a read on him and I just couldn't pin it down. I knew it was not a healthy situation for him.

## The Plan

When I lived in town with Farley, I did a lot of research about dogs, their behavior and their needs. I knew that Toby needed exercise as a healthy outlet for his energy. Once I established that in his life, I could start working on his behavioral issues. A plan started to formulate in the back of my mind. I fleshed it out and kept adding details. Then I waited for the opportunity to put my plan into action.

Toby hadn't been walked on a leash in years. The short skirmishes outside for potty breaks didn't count as walks. I knew it would be difficult working with him at first. He was a middle-aged dog with next to no leash training. He was also fear aggressive towards dogs and people he didn't know. For the plan to work, I had to make sure that he was under my control at all times.

Fortunately, Toby's leash was the standard cloth type. It was strong enough to hold him and easy for me to shorten or lengthen for different training purposes. He had a harness that I would attach a tether to, to secure him in the back seat of my car. I wouldn't use it to walk him because the purpose of using a harness on a dog is for it to pull. I didn't want to encourage Toby pulling me on walks.

For walking a dog, I prefer a martingale collar that allows for quick corrections with the sound of the snap without choking the dog. Timing is everything with this type of collar and it takes practice. I measured Toby's neck and bought a martingale collar that fit him. Toby already had a harness, and I still had the seat belt tether that I had used with Farley. I was ready. Then I waited.

## Car Rides and Walks!

One day my parents left the house for a few hours. I jumped on the opportunity to put the plan into action. I put a big, old towel on the back seat of my car and clicked in the seat belt attachment. I went back inside and put the harness and martingale collar on Toby, grabbed a bottle of water, a dish, and jammed treats and poopy bags into my pockets. I attached the leash to his collar, locked up the house as we left, and put Toby into the back seat of my car. I secured his harness, and we were ready to go.

I wasn't sure of where we were going, but that didn't matter. We were about to start a new phase of our life together. Car rides and walking on a leash. I ended up taking him to an industrial area. I could see there were no cars in the parking lot so I thought it was pretty safe to take him there.

When I let him out of the car he was excited, full of energy and nervous, all at the same time. I was really hoping this went well. He didn't understand the leash corrections I gave him, but my timing wasn't the best. He responded well to being rewarded with treats. Toby got lots of exercise, he explored a new place, and there were no triggers for his aggression. All in all, our first outing was a success.

We went back home. My parents came home later, and I told them what I had done. They were surprised and worried. I assured them that everything was fine and our first outing had gone well. They were nervous the first few times I took him out after that, but eventually, it became our regular routine. Toby lost weight, was more fit, and his energy level became more balanced over time.

I found three different industrial areas and two rural churchyards where I could walk Toby. We had great adventures on our walks. With practice, we both became better with the leash training. Eventually, if I had to give him minor corrections, he responded easily and willingly. We developed a flow and a rhythm.

Over time, he came to trust me completely. And over time, I saw him as a different dog. The nervous, tense, and aggressive dog was gone. Toby was now calm, relaxed, happy and playful. I was surprised to learn that his level of intelligence was so high. And then, he did have at least two types of herding breeds in his genetic makeup. I also came to know that he was very sensitive and respectful. I guess the right circumstances can bring out the best in anyone, dog or person.

## Progress

Before I started working with Toby, he was a live wired mess when people came to visit the house. He would frantically run around barking. It was so loud and annoying. At some point, he taught himself to pick up his rawhide stick in his mouth, run up the visitor, and then run away. Then he'd drop the rawhide, run around and bark. Over time, his behavior changed. Now he would bark once, greet them with his rawhide and then lie down. People started to comment on how much calmer he was. Hearing this made me feel very happy. Our training and walks were working. The benefits transferred to other areas of his life.

I think the places I found to walk Toby also helped me. They were filled with nature: trees, grass, and one had a creek running through the back. There were no people, traffic, loud noises or technology. The peace and quiet of these places helped me to connect with nature. And Toby, being an animal, was a part of nature.

Taking Toby to the veterinary hospital was not always calm and peaceful. He was fine at the hospital because he trusted everyone there. It was the drive to the hospital that could be a problem. If Toby saw a dog, he would aggressively claw at the car window while snarling and growling. I was driving so I couldn't intervene physically. I didn't yell at him because to me this would be the equivalent of another barking dog and that would have reinforced his behavior. I chose to talk calmly to him. Over time I would laugh, which really threw him off. He knew what laughter was and my reaction was a mismatch to his behavior.

And then in the last year of his life, as I was driving, I saw a dog. I calmly said, "It's okay" and made eye contact with Toby in the rearview mirror. I saw him look out the window at the dog. He barked once. Again I said, "It's okay." We made eye contact again in the rearview mirror. And that was the extent of his reaction. I was so proud of him and told him so. He had come such a long way with his behavior.

## The Wonder of Gas Stations?

If I needed to get gas and Toby was in the car, I would try to find a gas station that wasn't busy with customers. I was worried that he would bark like a fool and annoy other people. I based this on his reaction to seeing people walk across crosswalks.

Then one day, I really needed to get gas and the closest station was busy. I decided to take the risk of annoying other people with an out of control, barking dog. I pulled up to an empty pump and turned my car off. I was waiting for the loud barking to begin.

I looked in the rearview mirror and to my surprise, Toby couldn't turn his head fast enough in all directions to see everything that was going on around him outside of the car. He was so interested in all the activity. I have no idea why. This only happened at gas stations. I had accidentally found something that Toby enjoyed, so I added this to his life. Whenever I needed to get gas, I made sure it was after one of Toby's walks. It's the little things that make us happy in life.

## Familiar But New

I had told my best friend about a rural church that I would take Toby to for walks. It was isolated and most times no one was there. She asked if she and her boyfriend could meet us there and I agreed. I felt some trepidation in case Toby behaved badly with them. And then I remembered that my friend grew up on farms and was very comfortable with animals. And she had visited my parents' house a few times. Not a lot, but enough that Toby would probably remember her.

And he did, but not at first. I got Toby leashed up and out of the car. He didn't notice them at first because he was too busy sniffing all the new scents that had been put down since our last visit. My friend and her boyfriend were quiet. I gradually started walking Toby toward them. I think my friend said something and then Toby saw them. He started barking at them. I stood still and told him it was okay. My friend continued talking to him.

And then it happened. Toby made the connection. He knew this person. She wasn't a stranger. He couldn't get to her fast enough. He ran and dragged me up the hill to the benches they were sitting on. Toby was in heaven at a rural church. He was so happy and excited to greet them. He laid on his back and exposed his belly. That's trust for a dog. He couldn't get enough belly rubs and attention from them. This was one of the happiest and most fulfilling experiences I had with Toby, and I was grateful to my best friend for creating it.

## Health Problems

Toby had colitis for the last year and a half of his life. At first, I thought it was diarrhea but it wouldn't clear up. I tried changing his diet and nothing helped. The veterinarian treated him with tylosin, which worked initially, but over time it wasn't enough. We tried changing his diet several times, in case he was allergic to different proteins.

When you have a dog with colitis, you become an expert about the look and consistency of their stool. You also become adept at cleaning it up from the ground and off the dog's rear end. Toby had long fur on his back end and it was sometimes difficult to clean. When it was bad I used the scissors to cut his fur off. He may not have looked pretty, but I'm sure it was more comfortable for him.

I think his colitis was caused by the extreme stress in the household, due to my father's dementia. I told the veterinarian that and he said that animals were resilient and could handle a lot. Looking back on the intestinal problems I had after Toby died, I don't think people or animals have the resiliency to deal with the stress of dementia for a prolonged period of time.

Next, Toby's eyes were constantly red and watering. The veterinarian initially treated him for possible eye infections. It turned out to be allergies. I made a lot of visits to the veterinary hospital with Toby in his last year. He seemed to have one health condition after another, but that's a part of the aging process.

When I would get home with his new medications, I would write everything down on my calendar. What pills to give him and how many he would get in the morning, midday and at night. After I gave them to him I crossed it off on the calendar to keep track. I wanted so much for him to get better.

Getting him to take so many pills was not an easy task. There was a flavored paste that I got from the veterinarian to hide his pills in. This worked for a while. Then I became concerned because there was a protein source in this product and I didn't want it to increase his allergic response. I did some research on the internet and created my own paste. I used rice flour, olive oil, and bananas. This worked until Toby didn't want to eat anymore.

Next, I made bone soup for him to stimulate his appetite. The theory behind making bone soup is that cooking bones for a long time, twelve to twenty-four hours, leaches nutrients out of the bones. The soup is meant to be chocked full of these nutrients for healing. It wasn't until months after Toby died that I found out through an internet search that bone soup has no extra nutritional value. I could have saved myself a lot of time by just making chicken soup and using the broth as an appetite stimulant for Toby.

## Prey Drive

I was walking Toby in the winter at one of the industrial sites I took him to. I wasn't paying enough attention. I didn't see the frozen pigeon in the snow. Toby clamped down on it with his mouth. He was trying to eat it quickly. He knew from past experience that I would take it away from him. I was concerned that his eating this would trigger another bout of colitis.

I knew better than to put my hand near his mouth because he would bite me. I kept jerking on his leash back and forth, to and fro, to throw him off balance so he would drop the pigeon. It took a while, and he eventually dropped it. He was obsessed with it and I knew I had to get him away from it.

I practically dragged him to the car. I didn't read his behavior well. I forgot that he was an animal first, then a dog, then Toby. At the car, he was still the animal with a strong prey drive. I was moving too fast. I should have been more patient. I was reacting to my emotions and ignoring my intellect. I pushed him beyond his limits.

I opened the car door and moved toward him to help him jump into the back seat. He turned on me viciously. He meant business and would have attacked me if I hadn't moved away from him. I didn't blame him because I knew that I had not given him the time he needed to decompress. I was in too much of a hurry. I should have waited until the animal became the dog and then became Toby. I should have at least waited until the dog who understood and responded to commands was present.

And then I saw Toby. He looked at me with soft eyes and his behavior was submissive. He thought he had done wrong and I would reprimand him. That didn't happen. How could I correct him for being his true nature? I knew that this situation had turned out badly, and it was my fault. I did not correct, scold or reprimand him. When he was ready, I helped him into the back seat of my car and we continued on as usual. I think that over time Toby knew that I didn't hold grudges and I lived in the moment with him. I don't know any other way to be with a dog.

## A Change in Sleeping Arrangements

When I first moved into my parents' house, I noticed that Toby was very respectful of my space. He wouldn't go into my room unless I invited him to come in. Over time, his curiosity got the best of him. My room was directly across the hall from the bathroom. Sometimes when I came out of the bathroom, I would see Toby in or just leaving my room. When he saw me, he would quickly run out of the room. I always told him it was okay.

Throughout his life, he slept on the floor in my parents' bedroom. As my father's dementia progressed, I grew concerned for Toby's safety at night. My father had sundown syndrome which led to an increase in his confusion and restlessness at night. I was working, teaching classes, and I needed to sleep at night. Worrying about Toby was keeping me up at night.

I decided to train Toby to sleep in my room at night. This was not an easy task. Dogs are creatures of habit and Toby wanted to sleep where he knew to sleep. I started by luring him into my room with dog treats and then quickly closing the door behind him. I had to close the door quickly because he would try to run out of the room as soon as he had the dog treat.

It took a while for him to settle into this new routine. At first he was restless and would get up several times through the night. As time went by, he accepted his new bedtime location and routine. He came to enjoy it. I know that because he would run into my room at night and flop down on his bed. He was totally relaxed and would sleep soundly through the night.

## Degenerative Myelopathy

I got up on the morning of June first to feed Toby and take him outside to do his business. He wouldn't get up, as much as I tried to coax him. Finally, I had to leave to go to work. I kept calling home to see if he had got up yet but he just laid in the same place and position on the floor beside my bed. I knew something was wrong so I called the veterinary hospital and made an appointment. I left work. When I arrived home, I put Toby onto a quilt. My mother and I used the quilt to carry him out to my car.

Toby was diagnosed with degenerative myelopathy. The signals from the brain don't make it down the spinal cord to the back legs. The disease is progressive and eventually leads to paralysis of the hind legs. The only good thing about this disease is there is no pain involved for the dog. There is no cure.

As is my nature, when I got home I scoured the internet for any and all information about degenerative myelopathy in dogs. I found nothing that gave me hope, so I accepted his fate.

The veterinarian told me to keep him walking as much as I could to prevent muscle wasting. I knew I needed a device of some sort to support his back end while walking him. There were a lot of different harnesses that were expensive and some looked difficult to use. Then I saw that you could use a cloth shopping bag. You cut out the sides of it and use it as a sling to lift up and support the dog's back end. It worked!

As the disease progressed, Toby's mobility declined. I would use the shopping bag to lift him up and support his back end to get him outside to do his business. As time went by, I also used a body sling. Once I got him outside, I would hold the weight of his body with the sling while he did his business. When he finished, I would put the shopping bag back in place to help maneuver his back end to get him inside. Soon after, I needed to use the bag and sling to carry his whole body outside. He had become so weak that he didn't have the energy to use his front legs anymore.

## Harmony With Another Dog

Years before Toby's health problems with colitis and degenerative myelopathy, he had a lump that was growing quickly in size. Due to its location, the growth would eventually block his urinary functions. If left too long, it would have been impossible to remove and he would die. So, surgery it was.

When my mother and I went to pick him up after he'd recovered from surgery, I said something to the veterinarian about Toby's aggressive behavior toward other dogs. He told us that his dog had been around Toby all day while he was recuperating in the cage and Toby had been fine with her. He asked if we wanted to see this and I said yes. I found it hard to believe.

The veterinarian asked us to stand in the doorway. We did and saw Toby lying in a cage. When he saw us his eyes lit up and his tail wagged. The veterinarian whistled and his dog came out. She ran past the cage and Toby glanced in her direction and then looked back to us. He didn't react to her at all. At that moment, for me, seeing was believing.

And that moment stayed with me and gave me hope when I was working with Toby on our walks. I saw a part of him I'd only seen when he had been with Farley. I saw the potential in him.

I came to see that Toby always felt safe at the veterinary hospital with people and dogs. He never showed fearful or aggressive behavior when he was there. I never got him to the point where he could be with another dog and not react. With me, he improved to where he barked once when he was in the car and saw another dog. I thought that was as good as it was ever going to get until one of his last visits to the hospital.

The last few months with Toby had been hectic. With his colitis and lameness, I took him for many scheduled and some unscheduled visits. The visits are a blur in my memory. One blends into the next and I can't remember the specific details of each visit. I think it was the third or fourth last time I took him there, but I don't know for sure.

Toby was lying on the floor in the surgery room. He wouldn't walk for me. The veterinarian got him up and walked him with assistance. I was so frustrated that I was unable to do this for Toby. I had injured my back from lifting and carrying him so much. I was exhausted.

Toby was lying on the floor again and the veterinarian tried to give Toby either kibble or treats in an attempt to whet his appetite. He wouldn't eat them so the veterinarian put them on the floor in front of Toby. Then the veterinarian called for his dog to come out. I had no idea why he did this. I felt panic rising up in me. I was worried that Toby would hurt her.

I knew that how I reacted would affect Toby's behavior. I didn't want to transfer the energy of my emotions through the leash to Toby. I immediately calmed myself by going into a meditative state. The other dog came and stood beside Toby. I knew he lacked the mobility to move toward her, but she was right beside him and her face was close enough to his for him to bite her.

Toby glanced at her and then looked back at me. He only had eyes for me. He was calm and sedate, lying there with another dog standing beside him. This is what I had hoped for, for years. At first, I was stunned. I felt as though I was standing in timeless time. And then I was filled with gratitude. Farley was the only dog Toby had felt safe being near. And now, he felt that safeness again. I'm glad he had that experience one more time in his life.

# A Natural Death

## Nothing Left to Give

I took Toby to the veterinary hospital on the Monday before Labor Day. I was beside myself with worry for him. He was lethargic. I had to carry his whole body weight and I didn't know how much longer I could do that. With my back injured from carrying him so much, I was in constant pain. I was concerned that soon I wouldn't be able to help him.

He had been recently switched to a vegetarian or hypoallergenic dog food in the hopes that it would help his colitis. We changed his diet so many times, trying to find something that would help him. I can't remember which diet he was last on. The food had a more reddish color to it than the last food he was on. I noticed his stool had a red tinge and thought it was due to the diet change. That was what my intellect told me. My intuition said otherwise. I took a stool sample on this visit to the hospital. The veterinarian ran various tests.

The test results came back the next day. His blood work showed he was anemic. It was the stool sample that provided the answer. There was blood in Toby's stool. He was bleeding from his large intestine. It was probably the colitis, perhaps ulcerative.

I took him back in for iron and B12 injections. The goal was to boost his red blood cell count. He was also given an antibiotic injection to fight a possible infection and to help his bowels heal. Now it was a wait and see scenario. Hopefully, Toby's body would respond.

At the time I was still teaching my Tai Chi classes two nights a week out of town. When I got home from class on the Thursday night, I tried to take Toby out for a pee. It was a struggle for me. He was so weak that I had to carry his full weight. He and I were so stressed out that he wouldn't pee. I barely got him back into the house and into my room. I knew I'd reached the breaking point and couldn't continue this anymore. And I was concerned that I was forcing Toby to endure a poor quality of life.

We had an appointment the next day for the veterinarian to check on Toby's condition. The next morning I called and booked an earlier appointment to have Toby euthanized. I was torn. I thought this was best for Toby, and yet I had doubt. I scoured the internet for information on how to know when it's time to euthanize your pet.

I found an article that advised you to think of the five best things your dog likes to do. Toby's five best things were: chewing rawhide sticks, greeting people as they came into the house with a rawhide stick in his mouth, going for car rides where he sat up and looked out the window, watching people at the gas station, and most of all going for our long walks together. If your dog can no longer do three or more of these things, it is time to consider putting him down. Toby could do none of his best things anymore. This helped to confirm my decision, and yet doubt still niggled around in the back of my mind.

I called work and booked the day off. I arrived at the hospital early and just sat in the back of the car with Toby, saying my goodbyes and sharing the time we had left. This was the fourth time I had brought him to be euthanized over the last three months. You'd think I'd have been better at it with so much practice. That was not the case. Each time it pulled at my heart, and each time I made sure I was calm and collected so he would have a peaceful and gentle passing.

## Yes or No?

The veterinarian came out. He opened the back door, reached in and lifted Toby's upper lip to look at his gums and said, "I think he's pinking up." This meant that Toby's red blood cell count had probably improved. I turned my head away and muttered a curse word. I had not expected to hear this. The veterinarian carried Toby into the reception area of the hospital. Thank goodness, because I didn't have the strength to carry him.

The veterinarian checked a sample of Toby's stool and noted that it was not as red as the last time. This meant there was less blood loss. Then a woman came into the hospital. Toby lifted his head and looked at her. This was another good sign because it showed that his energy and strength had improved. And yet, I was undecided as to how to proceed. I didn't want to prolong Toby's suffering if there was no hope that he would survive.

The veterinarian said that he could give Toby a repeat of the injections to see if this led to further improvements. I told him that I needed to know for sure that Toby's anemia was improving, otherwise, I didn't see any point in continuing the treatment. The veterinarian suggested testing Toby's blood again to see if there was an improvement. I agreed to this because I needed to know.

The equipment at this hospital, to test the blood sample, was temporarily not working. The veterinarian took Toby's sample to another hospital to be tested. I sat on the floor with Toby in the reception area and waited.

A little while later, the veterinarian came through the front door and announced that there was a twenty percent improvement in Toby's red blood cell count. My heart skipped a beat. This was the first glimmer of hope I had allowed myself to feel since the previous night. Although I now had a faint glimmer of hope, I was still undecided. Toby had been through so much over the last year and a half. I didn't want to force him to endure needless pain and suffering.

The veterinarian suggested that we go outside to discuss Toby. He was trying to convince me to not euthanize Toby, to give Toby one more chance. I give him credit for advocating so strongly for his patient. I looked at him and asked, "In your professional opinion, with all of your years of experience and the results of the blood work, do you honestly think there is a chance that Toby can get better?" He replied yes, based on there being less blood in Toby's stool, Toby's ability to raise his head to look at the woman, and the improvement in his red blood cell count.

The veterinarian's answer to my question was a confirmation of what I knew to be the best for Toby. My decision was made. Toby would be coming home with me. Then I called my mother to ask if she agreed. This was a formality because I knew I would be bringing Toby home. The veterinarian gave Toby a repeat of the injections and then carried him to the car for me.

## Home Again

When I got home, I struggled to get Toby out of the car. I tried to find things to create a ramp to slide him off of the back seat of my car. I couldn't find anything that was sturdy enough for this. I ended up slowly lifting and lowering him to the ground using the quilt he was lying on. I used the sling and shopping bag to carry him over to the grass where he peed. Then I slowly and painstakingly carried him into the house and into my room.

I put the quilt under him because that was all I had for a quick makeshift bed. Later I went to a local Salvation Army store where they sell blankets and towels for one dollar each if they're to be used for pets. I bought five things because that's all they had. One was a beautiful, soft, thick duvet. I knew this would be the base of Toby's bed. It would cushion his body and hopefully reduce the chance of his getting pressure sores.

I folded the duvet to fit in the space on the floor beside my bed. The length, width, and depth of it was enough for Toby to lie on in comfort. I then laid the quilt on top of the duvet to complete his new bed. The other blankets and sheets I bought came into use later that weekend. I'm glad I purchased all these things, especially the duvet. Toby never left this bed.

## Give Him the Best

The veterinarian called me on Saturday to ask how Toby was doing. I told him that Toby had not moved at all. He had no energy and ate very little. The veterinarian said, "We're going to change the treatment plan." He told me to give Toby whatever he wanted. I asked what he meant by this. He said to give him whatever he wants to eat, chicken, cheese. I said it might bring his energy level up. The veterinarian said, "If these are his last days..." I finished his sentence with, "...give him the best." He agreed.

I went to the grocery store and bought chicken and expensive cheese for Toby. I cut both up into bite-sized pieces and offered them to Toby. He ate some and really liked it. He didn't eat a lot, but at least he ate something. I tried to feed him after that, but he wouldn't eat.

As the night progressed, he got weaker and weaker. I started giving him water out of his bowl. As time went by, he couldn't lift his head to drink. He would try to use his tongue out of the side of his mouth, but that didn't work well. I had to improvise.

I used a tightly folded blanket to prop his head so that his mouth was pointed downward. I placed pee pads under his head and around the area of his head. I poured the water into a tall, conical glass and held it at an angle so that Toby's tongue could easily lap the water. I kept pouring water into the glass until Toby finished drinking as much as he wanted to.

Toby and the pee pads were soaked. I removed the wet pads and replaced them with dry ones. Then I used a towel to dry Toby's face and head. This became our routine. He slept more and more, and for longer periods of time. Whenever he woke up, I gave him a drink.

## Go Pee

On Sunday morning, Toby was so tired and lethargic. I was concerned that he had not had a pee since Friday afternoon. I searched online for how to express a dog's bladder. I found a video where a veterinarian demonstrated how to do this. I watched it over and over until I thought I could do it. I tried it several times on Toby, but he wouldn't pee. He looked so uncomfortable and I felt bad for making him feel that way. He was so well trained that he wouldn't pee while inside the house.

I got down on the floor beside him, looked him in the eyes and said, "Toby, it's okay to go pee. You go pee." I repeated this several times. At first, he looked away from me. Then he looked me in the eyes and I knew he understood what I said. He closed his eyes. I saw his body relax and then he started peeing. I couldn't believe how much urine came out of him.

I kept putting more pee pads down. When he was done, I removed the wet pads and put clean ones under him. I had bought some non-allergic wipes for him. I used them to clean all the urine off of his fur. I had read that urine can cause skin burns if a dog is left to lay in it. I wanted him to be comfortable.

## Turning and a Turn

Throughout the weekend, I kept turning Toby's body from one side to the other to prevent pressure sores from forming. At first, this wasn't a problem. When I turned Toby on Sunday morning, there was no resistance in his neck. He had always shown resistance up to that point. I decided I wouldn't turn him anymore. It was too much for him. He was so tired and he had nothing left to give. That was when I knew he was dying. Now it was palliative and end-of-life care.

I let him sleep as much as he wanted and gave him water whenever he woke up. I tried to give him chicken and cheese, but he had no interest in food. Throughout the weekend I had been massaging his muscles and doing physiotherapy on his legs. I gave him Reiki and even said a Buddhist prayer of healing for him. I did everything I knew to do for him.

As Sunday progressed, Toby's breathing became more and more labored. As he inhaled his abdomen would expand, then quickly contract as he exhaled. He was in a deep sleep. That night I slept lightly and kept the bedside light on.

I woke up at 2:30 Monday morning to the sound of Toby's breathing. It was worse. It was louder and his abdomen was expanding and contracting at a faster rate. I sat on the floor beside him and ran my hands along his side to comfort him as best as I could. I kept talking to him, even though he was unconscious. This went on for hours.

And then he woke up. He was wide awake and alert. At first, I saw fear in his eyes. I moved quickly to sit on the floor beside his head to be close to him. He heard my voice first and then he made eye contact with me. I could see his body relax and his eyes fill with warmth.

I asked him if he wanted a drink and his eyes widened to acknowledge what I had said. I positioned his head and gave him a drink of water. I couldn't believe how much he drank. I just kept pouring water into the glass. When he was finished, I dried him off and put clean pads under him.

He immediately fell unconscious and his breathing became more labored. I sat on the floor beside him. I was caressing him with my hands and telling him it was okay. I told him he was smart, he was kind, he was gentle, and he was loved.

His abdomen violently convulsed a few times. Then his neck muscles convulsed once. He let out a deep breath and he was gone. The actual moment of his death seemed to happen so quickly. I was stunned at the abruptness of it. I couldn't believe he was gone. I continued to touch him for a few moments. I sat on my bed and looked at the clock. Then I sat for a while just looking at him. I felt lost.

Toby died on Labor Day Monday 2018, at 6:43 am.

## Support

After he died, I kept Toby's body in my room for about four hours. I had to hide the fact that he died from my father because I didn't know how my father would react to this news. I waited until my older brother came to help me break the news to our father. It went well.

My brother came to help me take Toby's body to an emergency care veterinary clinic. It was a holiday so the regular veterinary hospital was closed. My brother helped me to get Toby into the car and he drove us to the hospital. Oddly enough, the only time I cried that day was when I left Toby's body with them to be cremated. I felt like I was leaving him with strangers. That may not make sense, but emotions don't make sense to the intellect.

Toby's veterinarian and staff were great after his death. They called with condolences. Their receptionist was about to work her first shift at the hospital I had taken Toby's body to. The veterinarian called and asked if I wanted the receptionist to bring Toby's ashes to his hospital for me to pick up. I gratefully said yes. This veterinarian and his staff were so supportive. I didn't have that with Farley's death.

It's only now, just over a year after Toby's death, that I broke down crying while typing this. I have grieved his loss. I know this because I was relieved when he died. I knew his suffering was over. It's only now that I am dealing with the emotions that arose from the circumstances of his death. It would be normal to feel sad and cry when your pet dies. That was a luxury I was not afforded at the time of Toby's death.

Toby's death was the first time I'd experienced a natural death. I am grateful that he died alone with me. He knew he was safe and loved unconditionally. I believe that is the best way for any sentient being to die.

# Two Dogs, More Than One Grief

Toby's death was the impetus for my researching and writing about dying, death and the grieving process. I grieved his loss completely within three weeks of his death. Years later, I still carried what I thought was grief for Farley. I needed to understand why this was.

Throughout my life, I thought I knew what grief was. It was just a thing. It was something you experienced after you lost someone you loved and it involved feeling sad. Eventually, the sadness becomes softer over time until you are left with pleasant memories.

Now I know that it is so much more than that. There are different types of grief, and you can experience more than one type for a loss. There are also different factors and circumstances that affect the grieving process. It is much more complicated than I had originally thought. There are depths and levels of grief that I was unaware of.

In this chapter, I'll be sharing some of what I have learned about dying, death and grieving from my personal experiences and from the research I've done over the past year. I plan to expand on my research findings in a future book.

## The Different Types of Grief I Experienced

### Disenfranchised Grief

Disenfranchised grief happens when you feel unable to discuss what you have experienced with others because your loss is not acknowledged by society. Grieving the loss of a pet as a concept has become more known in our society, but I don't know if it has become accepted. Some people think that the loss of a pet is not as important as the loss of a person.

It makes it difficult when you hear comments like, "It was just a dog." Or, "When are you getting another one?" Some people bond more closely with their pets than others. And for some, their pet is the only being they have an emotional attachment to.

I experienced disenfranchised grief with Farley. I felt the need to talk about him, but that had never been done in my family with any other pets that died. We just didn't talk about it. I was able to talk to my best friend about it, but I felt our conversations were stilted and stunted. I didn't have the words to describe how and what I was feeling. My emotional vocabulary for grief was limited.

Years later when I told people I was writing a book on grieving the loss of pets, I was surprised at how open most people were about their own stories of loss. I initially thought people would be hesitant or reticent. Some were, but most people couldn't stop talking about it. It was as though they had finally found someone to share this important part of their life story with. There was no shame or holding back. It didn't matter if it happened two weeks ago or twenty years ago. People wanted to talk about how important their pet was to them, and how much it hurt them when their pet died.

## Complicated Grief

I thought I had experienced complicated grief after Farley died. Normal grief lasts a few weeks to a few months. What I experienced after losing Farley lasted for many months. With complicated grief, the feelings of loss don't go away and this interferes with moving on with your life. It can last for months or years. It can also be severe enough to require medical and psychiatric treatment.

I realize now that I carried feelings of guilt while grieving the loss of Farley. This exacerbated my grief. I felt guilt over having gone to work that day when I knew something was off about him. I also felt guilt over his having to be injected twice in his heart before he died. I now know that I did the best I could for him, and everything else that happened on his last day was due to circumstances beyond my control.

## Anniversary Grief

This is a common type of grief. The first anniversary of the loss is the hardest. For the first five anniversaries of Farley's death, I went to the seven o'clock movie at the local theatre so I didn't have to think about him. Fortunately, The Lord of the Rings movies were playing for most of those.

I didn't go to the theatre on the anniversary after Toby died. I didn't feel the need to not think about Farley on that anniversary, and I know I will never need to again. And I didn't do anything to avoid thinking about Toby on the first anniversary of his death. I chose to reflect on the good feelings and memories I had of him.

Toby's death changed me and how I grieve about pets. I think it's because I knew I did everything possible to help him. I have no regrets. Perhaps that is the lesson he was meant to teach me. I was finally able to apply this lesson to my thoughts and feelings about Farley.

## Anticipatory Grief

This is a type of grief that prepares you for what is to come. People experience this when a loved one is ill for a long time prior to death. It is common when a loved one has reached the point of needing palliative care or is living in a hospice.

I experienced this with Toby. I grieved so many of his losses in the last year and a half of his life. He lost some of his health to colitis. Then he lost the ability to walk. And then he lost more of his health when he became anemic. I think grieving these lesser losses along the way prepared me to grieve the loss of his life.

## Normal Grief

Again, this is the one that lasts for a few weeks or a few months. You are able to work through your feelings and emotions in a way that is healthy and healing. Then you can move forward and live your life well.

I also experienced this type of grief with the loss of Toby. I think experiencing a natural death helped me with this. I didn't see it as a fearful or ugly experience. After I had time to contemplate what had happened, I found the experience of his death to be beautiful.

## Factors and Circumstances That Affected My Grief

The factors and circumstances that I am writing about were specific to me and the grieving process that I experienced with Farley, and then Toby. There are many other factors and circumstances that can affect grief and grieving.

## Bonding

Farley was a part of my daily life for over fourteen years. I had a very strong bond with him. Toby was a part of my life for five and a half years. The bond I had with him was not as strong. That didn't make Toby any less important to me. Our relationship was different from the one I had with Farley.

## Emotional Investment

Looking back, I know that I was overly attached to Farley. And through my research, I've learned that can happen with some people. I have no regrets about this, and I have learned to not become emotionally attached to a pet in an unhealthy way. It is healthy to have a balance and moderation in all areas of your life.

With Toby, I kept myself more emotionally distanced from him. I loved him and took care of all of his needs. I made sure I stayed balanced emotionally. I had learned from grieving Farley's death.

## Unexpected Versus Gradual Death

Farley's death was unexpected for me. I knew that he was an older dog and his time was coming. I didn't expect his death on that day. I went to work and he was walking on his own. I came home in the afternoon and he had suffered two strokes and couldn't walk.

With Toby, his decline was gradual. First health problems, then lameness. Grieving the different losses in his life brought me gradually closer to grieving his death.

## The Veterinarian

The veterinarian who performed Farley's euthanasia was new and unknown to me. For this reason, I had not developed a sense of trust in him.

I had known Toby's veterinarian for many years. He was also Farley's veterinarian for the first nine years of his life. I trusted this doctor completely. That made a big difference for me.

## Euthanasia Verses a Natural Death

Farley was my first and only dog that was euthanized. This was a new experience for me. It seemed so sudden and cold.

Toby was the first dog that I had witnessed having a natural death. Being with him, caring for him, and comforting him as best as I could was deeply fulfilling. If at all possible, I would choose a natural death for a pet. And I would choose to be there with them.

## Veterinary Support

With Farley, I think we received a sympathy card from the veterinary clinic. That was nice, but Farley wasn't a regular patient of theirs and we hadn't established a rapport with them. I didn't feel any support from them, and I didn't expect any.

With Toby, it was very different. I had known the veterinarian and his staff for many years. First with Farley, and then with Toby. I got to know them better with Toby because I was there so often with his medical appointments. The support they gave me after Toby died helped me a great deal with the grieving process. It let me know that

Toby mattered and he had touched the lives of people in meaningful ways.

## Experience With Grieving

When Farley died, I had no experience with grieving the loss of a pet that I was bonded to. I was adrift in a sea of unknowns. When Toby died, I could draw on the lessons that I had learned from grieving Farley's death.

## Private Versus Public Grief

I didn't feel comfortable publicly expressing my grief after Farley died. I wanted to, but it felt so awkward. After Toby died, I talked about it to everyone and anyone who would listen. The pay off was that people responded in kind. This helped me a lot and was a good life lesson for me.

## Things That Helped Me While Grieving

### Talking About it With Others

Talk to a friend, a family member, a grief counselor or join a pet loss support group. An important part of the grieving process is verbalizing your thoughts and emotions. It helps you to identify what you are feeling. And it just feels good to get it out and share with others. It's a way to feel connected when you are going through a difficult time in your life.

### Journaling or Writing

The writing process has helped me to process what happened and how I felt about it. Rather than just having feelings inside, it allowed me to identify what I was feeling and why I was feeling it. It felt like a journey of self-discovery.

## Spirit Walks

After Farley and Toby died, I would walk where I had walked them when they were alive. This helped me to process my grief. I would have flashes of memories from our walks. I felt sad and the walking helped me to move through the sadness. Each walk helped me to release a part of my grief.

When the happy memories came more often than the feelings of sadness and loss, I knew I was well on my way to healing. Eventually, I didn't feel the need to take these walks. That's when I knew I was ready to move on.

## Music

With each death, I found that music helped me to balance the energy of my mind, body, and spirit. I listened to very different types of music after the death of each dog. I think it had to do with balancing the yin or yang energies.

I learned that there was one type of music that I always listened to at the end of the grieving process. It was classical music. When I reached the point where I could peacefully listen to classical music, I knew I was balanced physically, mentally, emotionally and spiritually. I could feel the emotional changes and vibrations of the music in every cell of my body and every fiber of my being. If I was not at or near the end of the process, I would feel antsy and didn't have the patience to listen to it.

## Connecting With Your Spirit or Spirituality

I have been a Buddhist for over thirty years. I was fortunate to have a martial arts teacher who was also a Buddhist priest. I learned more from him that I could have learned from books or the internet.

When a person or a dog in my life dies, I say prayers for their soul for forty-nine days to help the soul cross over. I especially remember to do it for dogs because Sensei said that the worst ghost is a dog ghost. I don't know what he meant by that or if it's true, but I don't want to take any chances. I say prayers for the souls of the dogs that I have lost. Spiritually, this is important to me.

## The Surge of Yang Energy

I'm including this part for Buddhists, practitioners of Traditional Chinese Medicine and scholars who may find it of interest. I've learned something new from my personal experiences. I was not able to find much information to explain what I experienced. This is a topic I plan to research further in the future.

Just prior to Toby's death, I felt a surge of energy. I have been working with energy for many decades with the Tai Chi, Qigong, and Reiki. This was different from anything I had ever experienced. My energy level increased significantly. It has since leveled off, but it continues at a higher level than I have ever had in my lifetime.

I've learned that the soul is yang energy and the physical body is yin energy. When the soul is preparing to leave the body (death), there is a surge of yang energy which helps the soul to separate from the body.

It is common knowledge in hospices that this happens about two days before a person dies. The person becomes more energetic and animated. Unfortunately, this gives their loved ones false hope that this person is recovering.

I have not been able to find information about the surge of yang energy in dogs or birds, but I experienced it with each. When Toby was dying, I first thought it occurred when his labored breathing woke me early in the morning. Now I know that it was when he woke up for his last drink of water. He went from being completely unconscious to being wide awake and alert. So for dogs, the surge of yang energy happens a few minutes before death.

For the bird, the time between the surge and death is much shorter. Sparks, the budgie I made a nest for to sleep in my bed after her stroke, died while I was sleeping. The surge of yang energy allowed her to move enough to get under my right palm on the pillow. I awoke and found her dead under my palm. I think it was the surge of yang energy that awoke me. For her, this must have occurred within seconds, or at most a minute, before she died.

# Afterward

## Perfect Storm

Two months after Toby died, I realized I was always rushing to take care of him around work, classes, and dementia. I have no regrets. I would have done everything the same and more to have helped Toby regain his health. It was not meant to be. It was his time.

I've always believed that if you work hard enough and push through difficult times you will succeed, eventually. That had been true in my life up until the past year or so. Now I believe that is true most of the time.

In the months leading up to Toby's death, I was dealing with a parent at home with dementia, working five days a week at a small company that was going through major changes, teaching classes two nights a week out of town, and trying to fit in numerous and often unexpected visits to the veterinary hospital with Toby. I was exhausted, moving from one crisis to the next at home and at work.

The two things that kept me sane were Toby and teaching my classes. Unfortunately, Toby's health continued to decline and the classes I'd taught for twenty-six years were losing money.

It was a perfect storm of stressors due to circumstances beyond my control. I did everything I knew to do from my past life experiences. That was not enough because everything was new and untested. My health suffered as a result. At one point, for a while, I didn't know if or when I would recover. Even the doctors didn't know for sure what was happening in my body.

I've learned that chronic stress causes the body to release a flood of stress hormones. If the stress continues, the body's natural mechanisms to turn off this release stop working. This created serious health problems for me. Eventually, the prolonged stress also affected my cognitive functioning. I was in no-man's-land. I didn't know how to navigate in this new territory or where to navigate to.

I've since made changes in my life to reduce the stressors. And some stressors came to their natural conclusion. As a result, I have regained my health, and in some ways I feel better than ever.

The natural mechanisms that turn off the release of stress hormones are working again. I've calmed my body and mind and reconnected them to the point where I can meditate. I now feel the need to be social and reconnect with people. And the last thing I'm working on is brain training to create new neural pathways to improve my cognitive functioning. My sitting here typing what I'm thinking and feeling tells me this is working.

I'd always considered myself a strong person until the events of the past year. The storm nearly broke me. And yet here I sit at my desk writing my first book. My thoughts are clear and I'm able to find the words to describe and explain what I experienced. What a gift. I am grateful for all that has happened. I have found new strengths within me that I didn't know existed. And there are parts of me that I choose to let go of, as they no longer serve a purpose in my life.

I remember Sensei saying that life lessons are repeated until you 'get' them. If you ignore a lesson, it gets stronger or more difficult the next time. It's the universe's way of hitting you over the head when you don't pay attention. Now I've learned the lessons I needed to learn and can move on to new lessons. There's always something new to learn.

## The Animals

After Toby died, animals, domestic and wild, behaved differently toward me. The first experience I had was hiking in a conservation area. I could see two women and a Border Collie walking toward me on the path. I saw that the dog was hesitant and nervous when it saw me.

It's hard to put into words. It's as though everything that I've learned in my lifetime about animals and their behavior has come together as a body of information in my mind. It's like a database that I tap into without thinking about it.

This dog paused, put its head down and slowed its walk in my direction. It would look at me and then look away to avoid eye contact. It put its head down and its body lowered slightly into a creeping walk.

I intuitively stepped to the side of the path with my body facing away. This seemed to relax the dog and motivate its curiosity. I slightly extended the back of my left hand to it. The dog gingerly walked up to me and sniffed my hand. I saw its body relax even more. I started gently talking to it and then proceeded to pet it. By the end, I was running my hands along its back.

Then one of the women said in a stern voice, "This dog NEVER goes up to strangers!"She was pretty adamant and her comment sounded like an accusation. I wasn't sure what I should say or do. So I said, "Have a nice day," and continued on my hike.

The next experience was later in the fall. I was sitting on the back step of the house. I saw movement at the top of the hill in the farmer's field. I knew it was an animal, but it was too far away for me to see it clearly. It was making its way diagonally across the field in my general direction.

It kept stopping and looking to its right. This was the direction of the neighbor's backyard and I sensed it was checking to make sure the dog was not out. As it came closer I saw that it was a red fox with something black in its mouth. I was surprised because I had lived in this area for most of my life and had rarely seen a fox. I'd never seen one this close.

It continued on its diagonal path and then it veered directly toward me. There was a fence at the edge of the field. The fox stood on the other side of the fence, staring directly at me. I saw that it was holding a dead black squirrel in its mouth. It stood there for a few minutes staring directly into my eyes.

I was spellbound and mesmerized. I felt profoundly at peace as we looked into each others' eyes. I felt as though I was looking into its soul and it into mine. Then it broke off its gaze, turned around and continued across the field on its original diagonal path. I had the sense that it specifically changed its intended course to come and look at me. It was an odd and meaningful experience for me.

The third animal experience involved a young raccoon. It was the spring of the next year and I was standing in the alcove outside of the front porch door. I was on my cell phone talking to my best friend. I saw movement under one of the vehicles in the driveway. It was just after sunset so it was difficult to see with the lack of light.

Then it came out from under the vehicle, stood still and stared at me. I was surprised that it was so close to me. I told my friend and she was upset. She told me to avoid it because this was not the normal behavior of a wild animal and it might be sick. I told her it looked healthy, and she insisted it was not normal behavior.

I crouched down to a squatting position as I continued to talk on the phone. It would tentatively come toward me and then circle away. It did this several times as it gradually moved closer and closer to me. I was in awe at its proximity to me. My friend, on the other hand, was getting upset by my commentary of the raccoon's movements. I kept my body still and relaxed, and continued talking. I realized the raccoon was very young and curious.

Then he was so close to me I could have easily touched him. I thought it best not to. And then he touched his nose to my left knee. I stayed still and relaxed. He touched my knee three times with his nose. When he finished checking me out, he turned and walked away under the vehicle to where ever raccoons go to at night.

The last experience I had was this past summer. I had been working on my other book at a coffee shop. As I was exiting the shop, I saw a woman with two small dogs on leashes. She was standing still while talking to someone on her cell phone. I could see the dogs were nervous as they tensed their bodies and walked as far away from me as their leashes would allow.

I stopped and waited for the woman to make eye contact with me. When she did, I asked her if I could pet her dogs. She said yes. She also said that they probably won't bite, but the one would probably bark and growl at me. I said okay.

I squatted down, stayed still, averted my eyes and extended the back of my left hand. The one who could have been aggressive was the braver one who came up to me first. He slowly approached. He would stop and look at me. When he saw that I was not moving or talking, he would come closer. Then he came close enough to sniff my hand. This gave the other dog courage. She came over and sniffed my hand, too. She quickly became bored with my company and walked away. The other dog stood beside me.

I heard the woman talking to the person on the other end of her telephone conversation. She said, "Oh, you will never believe this. So and so (I can't remember the male dog's name) walked right up to a stranger and didn't bark or growl. He's standing calmly beside her right now."

Then a man and woman came out of the coffee shop. The woman started talking to the dog in a high pitched, loud voice, the way some people do when they talk to a dog or a baby. At first, I thought this might trigger the dog's nervous or fearful behavior, but it didn't. He just calmly stood beside me, looked at the woman and then looked away.

Intellectually, I want to understand why animals are drawn to me since Toby's death. I would especially like to understand why the wild animals came close to me, without fear and filled with curiosity. This was new to me. I've lived in rural areas most of my life and I know it's not normal for this to happen.

My first thought is they were attracted to the high levels of adrenaline in my body. I don't know if this would have a smell, but animals have a much keener sense of smell than humans. Since my body has recovered from the effects of prolonged stress, I have not had any more experiences with wild animals. Maybe it was the adrenaline, and maybe not. I don't know and maybe I never will. I may never understand or experience it again, but I know I will always treasure the memories of those encounters.

The experiences I have had with dogs, since Toby's death, are easier to understand. Having spent so much time with a dog who was extremely fearful and expressed that fear as aggression, I'm probably better able to see the nuances in the behavior of dogs as they become tense or nervous. I see and sense this before a full out behavioral outburst.

Also, being around Toby I learned to remain calm and confident during his explosions. This took time and practice for me. Eventually, I learned that my behavior would either quickly escalate or slowly calm his behavior. I chose the latter.

I used to feel the need to connect with nature through animals. This was intentional and deliberate on my part. It was as though I was forcing myself on them. Now I wait for them to come to me in their time, if they want to. I'm not offended in any way if they do not want to come to me. The connection I feel now just happens naturally, without intention or deliberation. The energy flows from one living being to another.

Intuitively, I know that I have changed in some way. It might be that I have a greater appreciation for life after all that I've been through. Perhaps it's due to a combination of things, some of which I am not yet aware of. Whatever caused this change, I am grateful for it. I feel a deeper connection with nature, and especially with animals. I accept this as a new reality and part of my life.

## Cooper

Cooper is an old Golden Retriever. He and his owner, Janice, used to live beside my workplace. When I first saw her walking him, I was drawn to him. His calm, relaxed and easy going nature brought his owner and I together in friendship. Dogs have a way of doing that, bridging relationships between strangers. I had no way of knowing at the time that this would be an important relationship for both Janice and I.

Over the past few years, I would apartment and pet sit for her. She also has an elderly cat named Oscar. Getting away from dementia for a day or two, every now and then, was an oasis for me. And having animals in my life after Toby died helped me to move through the grieving process with greater ease.

Recently, Cooper stayed with me for two weeks while Janice was away on vacation. His gentle and quiet nature makes him a perfect house mate. He taught me to slow down a little more, which gave me the opportunity to re-learn how to completely relax. His presence was what I needed to end my healing journey.

I took Cooper to one of the rural churchyards that I used to take Toby to. It was a different kind of spirit walk for me. One moment I would feel a pang of sadness from a memory of Toby, and the next moment I was filled with the joy of being with Cooper. It was a blending of the old and new.

There is life after death and grieving.

Out of aaalll the puppies in the world, Farley is the best.

# About the Author

DEBRA BILTON has had pets for most of her life. She had studied the behavior of dogs, learning theories, and techniques and methods to train and help them. In addition to studying psychology and education, she has studied the martial arts for forty years. She had been teaching Tai Chi and other internal martial arts for twenty-seven years. She is also a Buddhist.

Email: 2dogs2griefs@gmail.com

Website: www.2dogs2griefs.com

www.ingramcontent.com/pod-product-compliance
Lightning Source LLC
Chambersburg PA
CBHW070755250726
48662CB00004B/1816